Essential Jo

Comprehensive techniques and 2-person drills
for the Japanese 4-foot staff

Dan Djurdjevic

4th Dan, Chief Instructor, Academy of Traditional Fighting Arts

Pikkeljig Press

First published 2015

Pikkeljig Press
PO Box 388
Bayswater 6933 Australia

www.pikkeljig.com

Cover photograph by Lucia Ondrusova
Interior photographs by Lucia Ondrusova and Nenad Djurdjevic

ISBN-13: 978-0-9925113-3-3
Disclaimer: Martial arts practice is dangerous. Any advice given in this book is not intended to be a substitute for teaching by a qualified martial arts instructor. While the information in this book is true and complete to the best of the author's knowledge, the techniques and methods described in this book could lead to injury or death – whether performed correctly or not. All recommendations in this book are therefore given without any guarantee on the part of the author or publisher. No liability is accepted for any injury or damage as a result of the use or misuse of any data or specific details in this book.

This work is dedicated to my wife Maureen, for her tireless support, assistance and encouragement.

CONTENTS

1. INTRODUCTION

What is the jo?

The jo is a staff that is approximately 4 feet in length, used in Japan by the samurai as an adjunct to their kenjutsu (sword fighting skills using the katana). Indeed, traditional samurai schools like Tenshin Shoden Katori Shinto Ryu still teach the techniques of the katana and jo side by side: they teach sword drills, jo drills and sword vs. jo drills.

The art of "jodo" (the way of the jo) presented in this book is primarily based on the aikijo method (the jo method taught by aikido founder Morihei Ueshiba). I studied this art with my teacher Bob Davies and (occasionally) directly with his aikido teacher, the late Ken Cottier. Ken was a very senior British aikidoka and a direct student of Ueshiba.

I say that our jo method is "primarily" based on aikijo since it has been influenced by my other studies, notably:

- Tenshin Shoden Katori Shinto Ryu (to which I was also introduced by Bob Davies); and

- the Chinese internal and external weapons arts of Chen Pan Ling as taught by my teacher, his son Chen Yun Ching Shifu.

In terms of the latter, I've found the dynamics of Chen Pan Ling's walking stick form and his "xingyi kun" (a rattan 6-foot staff based on the internal art of xingyiquan) to be very similar to that of the aikijo and these have left a subtle, but important, imprint on my jo technique.

Origins of the jo

Legend has it that the techniques for the jo were invented by a 17th century samurai, Musō Gonnosuke Katsuyoshi after he fought a duel with Japan's most famous swordsman, Miyamoto Musashi. Accounts vary, but it is said that Gonnosuke met Musashi somewhere between 1608 and 1611, either at Edo or Akashi. At the time, Musashi was busy carving a bow out of piece of willow. Without warning Gonnosuke attacked Musashi with a wooden sword or staff (again, accounts vary).

Musashi easily deflected the attack using the piece of willow and knocked Gonnosuke to the ground.

After his defeat Gonnosuke went into seclusion at a Shinto shrine, determined to discover a means of defeating Musashi using a staff. It is said that following a divine experience, Gonnosuke changed the length of his staff from that of a sword (approximately 100 cm) to the length of the present-day jo (approximately 128 cm).

He then invented techniques appropriate for a weapon of that length.

A representation of famed Japanese swordsman Miyamoto Musashi

Some say that Gonnosuke went on to fight a second match with Musashi, defeating the latter using his longer jo, however this is disputed.[1]

The Muidokan jo method

We call our school the Academy of Traditional Fighting Arts, however its Japanese name is "Muidokan" (in Chinese "Wu-Wei Dao Guan") – the "house of the way of least resistance". This reflects both our philosophical and technical emphasis of avoiding unnecessary action by "going with the flow" and using the attacker's force against him or her.

The Muidokan jodo syllabus is set out in the Appendix at the end of this book.

At the core of our jo method are a series of 20 basic techniques called "suburi" (see Chapter 3). We have retained these from aikijo as we find them to be a comprehensive catalogue of the different jo deflections, strikes and sweeps.

---

[1] See http://en.wikipedia.org/wiki/Muso_Gonnosuke and http://en.wikipedia.org/wiki/J%C5%8D.

Bob Davies – my first teacher

Added to this are 9 "kumijo" (literally "a meeting of jos") – 2-person combat drills that apply the suburi in a dynamic, effective environment (see Chapter 4). These drills are modeled on traditional kumijo from various schools but are, in the end, my own creation. They are the result of more than 30 years of martial training, combining the features of the arts to which I refer above, and many other armed and unarmed disciplines.

Importantly, unlike many other 2-person drills taught in relation to the jo and other weapons, the drills presented in this book "loop": that is to say, they can be practised continuously without end. The practical result of this is that in each drill both sides use the same sequence. The sequences are also short (between 6 to 10 movements), making them easy to learn.

The "looping" nature of these drills is not just a means of facilitating inculcation. Nor is it merely a matter of learning/teaching convenience. Rather, each move has been carefully thought through so that it provides the most logical and economic answer to the attack you are facing. The drill then provides your partner with the best answer to your counter. And so it goes. Like the game of "rock, paper, scissors", these drills cycle through the optimum responses to various attacks, "grooving" effective, reflexive responses, which utilize "wu-wei" – the Daoist concept of "no unnecessary action" or the "line of least resistance".

The 9 kumijo provide what I feel are a comprehensive set of jo skills. It is my experience that when you've well and truly inculcated these drills into your reflexive response, you will have an answer to virtually every type and angle of attack.

Chen Yun Ching – my current teacher

Add to this the traditional 13 count jo form (which is, in itself, a sophisticated 2-person drill) and the 31 count form (which is an exercise in learning the graceful flow of this weapon) and you have what I believe is both a complete system of civilian defence as well as an elegant art form.

The purpose of this book is to give a detailed and comprehensive account of the suburi and kumijo. It is my belief that these can be usefully adopted as an adjunct into the syllabus of any martial arts school. In this regard the book can serve as both a training aid and as an instructor's resource (particularly when used in conjunction with the forthcoming companion DVDs).

The "usefulness" of jo training

But why the jo? Why should a martial artist be concerned with this weapon when there are so many others one might choose to study? One answer to this question lies in the nature of the stick – the first and simplest of tools acquired by man – and its primeval connection to our psyche.

In our school we teach students how to handle three lengths of stick, not only for the above reason but because the stick (in whatever form) is probably the most likely object you are going to have on hand in a civilian defence scenario.

Initially we teach the baton (short stick), then the jo (medium stick), then the 6-foot staff (long stick). Of the three I feel the jo length is the most commonly found amongst everyday tools and implements: most brooms, rakes or other gardening implements are approximately the "jo length".

Furthermore the techniques of the jo translate almost as well to a walking cane or umbrella. In short, I feel that the jo is probably the most useful "stick weapon" to learn for civilian defence.

What is so special about the jo is that it combines the best of all worlds in terms of sticks: It is light enough to be wielded with one hand (although this is not where its primary "magic" lies). It can be used like a katana - yet it can also be flipped and used "end to end".

Unlike the 6-foot staff (known as the kon/bo), you can readily use a grip that is biased to one side (where typically Japanese/Okinawan kon/bo systems tend to use an even grip at the thirds). But like the kon/bo, you can also grip it at the thirds (if circumstances require it).

In short, it is a weapon for all occasions.

The versatility of the jo is such that it is even used by some police force units in Japan, particularly by those working in large open areas (eg. airports – see the picture below).

And like any stick, the jo amplifies your movements. This is both a blessing and a curse. When you make a mistake, it is apparent for all to see. In sparring you know when you've miscalculated. You just know you're going to "cop it" and there is no escape.

On the other hand, when you get things right, you can look downright marvelous. Such is the nature of the jo: there are no "in-betweens". It is a hard mistress, but a generous one as well.

Finally there is a very pragmatic reason for any martial artist to train in weapons – in particular the stick variety: the tip of a stick travels much faster than the hand or foot ever can. Accordingly, training with a stick can force your hand/body/eye coordination to experience, and manage, high speed attacks.

And if you can deal with fast attacks of this nature, you will be able to manage anything slower far more easily than if you did not have this exposure.

The types of jo

The traditional jo in Japanese martial arts is made of hardwood. Often it is tapered at the ends, however this is not always the case.

An airport police officer in Japan carrying a jo

My own beloved jo is of the non-tapered variety and is made of Japanese red oak, a comparatively light hardwood. It has withstood 2 decades of bashing and smashing and is still going strong.

For day-to-day use, I highly recommend the Chinese version of this staff – typically made of a type of bamboo called rattan. The advantage of the rattan jo is that it tends not to fail catastrophically after repeated hard contact.

On this subject I will issue this caution: Don't go out and buy a broomstick from your local hardware shop and bring it to the dojo for practice. While it may well be more conveniently and cheaply acquired than a purpose-made jo, it provides a false (and dangerous) economy. I speak from experience. When I first opened my own dojo I went out and bought a whole pile of pine sticks for my students to use. Midway through the first lesson shards of sharpened pine started whizzing past our heads as the sticks failed in the most spectacular way. But for dumb luck one of us would have lost an eye. So don't mess around: buy a proper jo.

Traditional hardwood jos are made of a very dense wood that tends not to break very easily. Sometimes these jos are regularly treated with oil such as linseed to keep the wood supple and less prone to catastrophic failure.

An example of a hardwood jo

As for the idea that you should use a heavy jo to build strength, my advice is that your time is far better spent acquiring skill than risking repetitive strain injury with a jo that is too heavy. If you want to build muscle, go to the gym.

An example of a rattan jo

The rattan jo is probably the safest: it doesn't "break" after repeated impact. Rather it tends to become stringy and limp at the end of its "life". This is both a benefit and a drawback. If you want a weapon to last a lifetime (or at least a couple of decades, as my Japanese red oak jo has) then the rattan jo isn't going to cut it. A rattan jo will only last a matter of months (assuming regular, frequent training with "stick on stick" impact).

But on the other hand, rattan jos are relatively inexpensive compared to their hardwood alternatives: they can be anywhere up to 10 times cheaper.

Just don't try to treat your jo with linseed or any other oil; I've seen people try it and the result isn't pretty (unless you like a stick that swells like a dead fish).

Rattan jos are also suitably light, something I see as another "winning feature". Most people I know start with a heavy jo in the mistaken belief that it gives them more "firepower". In explaining their preference they also cite the fact that they want to develop their arm and hand strength.

On the "power" side, I'll make this observation based on years of practical experience with the jo and other stick weapons: the speed of your stick provides the major component of the force applied by it — and this speed more than off-sets any lack of weight. Conversely, while a heavy stick might pack a lot of "power", this is of little use against a faster, more easily manipulated weapon. You'll simply be "beaten to the punch".

In the end it is a matter of taste: I have my old Japanese red oak jo (which I lovingly reserve for solo work and the occasional hard training). For day-to-day use I have a rattan jo. When it wears out, I'll buy another.

To summarise, I strongly endorse buying a proper, lightweight jo – specifically a rattan one – for reasons of both safety and practicality.

2. THE BASICS

Informal grip

As with golf, tennis, or any other activity which requires using a stick-like object, your grip is one of the most important features.

The "informal grip" is one you adopt when you are not actively engaged in training. We use the traditional method also seen in other Japanese and Chinese weapons arts: the weapon is held palm down and behind your shoulder.

This is not only subtle and non-confrontational; it also provides an element of concealment and surprise, should you need it against would-be assailants.

Surprisingly, the hold is also quite effective in allowing a "quick draw" for defence.

The informal grip – side view

The informal grip – front view

The key to this "quick draw" is to hold the jo slightly off-centre, palm closer to the end facing downwards.

I've found that the ideal point is approximately one palm width from the centre (or slightly less than that).

What this means is that when you drop the jo naturally it slopes upwards at a gradual incline – an incline that permits you, where necessary, to jab the jo forwards at an attacker so that it follows a straight line directly to your opponent's eye (or face generally).

In other words, if you have the correct bias to your grip, your relaxed thrust will not have any "upwards scoop". All this can be achieved without any effort or muscular exertion – merely by having the right grip.

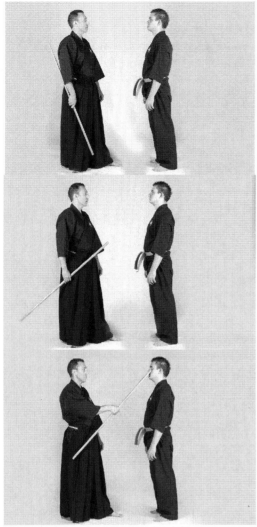

The informal grip used in defence

The "rule of quarters"

I have a rule that I follow in terms of handling the jo – a rule that I call "the rule of quarters". This is because, apart from the informal grip referred to above, I believe that the jo should principally be held with one hand at the end, and the other at the quarter marker closest to that end.

When you slide the jo through your hands you generally move one hand up to the ¾ mark, then swap ends.

I'll detail this further on in relation to the hand changes. It is sufficient for the present purposes to note that the quarter markers are significant. In order to isolate these, grab the jo exactly in the middle, then find the midway point from the middle to the end. This will be where one of your hands should grip, while the other goes to the end.

The "rule of quarters"

The thrusting grip

The basic grip at the conclusion of a thrust is performed in accordance with the "rule of quarters": your right hand is at the butt, while your left hand is at the nearest quarter point.

Both hands grip the jo naturally and in a relaxed fashion. In this respect it is important to note that except at the point of impact the jo is never gripped too tightly.

The thrusting grip

It is important to remember that in the first part of the movement (the slide) you are not moving your front arm forward – all that is happening is that you are sliding your jo through your front hand to the ¼ position (in accordance with the "rule of quarters" as described above).

After you have finished sliding to the ¼ position" you should throw your front arm into your thrust (keeping your thrusting grip at the ¼ mark firm).

The striking grip

The basic grip at the conclusion of a strike is also performed in accordance with the "rule of quarters". However in this case your left hand is at the butt of the jo while your right hand is at the nearest quarter point (with a slightly different grip – more on that in a moment).

The striking grip

The "slide then jab" principle

In the coming chapters, I will frequently make reference to something I call "slide, then jab". This is the central principle for thrusting with the jo as it ensures the appropriate staged activation, which in turn delivers optimum transfer of momentum and accordingly maximum application of force to your target.

Under this principle you must thrust in exactly this sequence:

1. Slide your jo to the ¼ position (ie. to the thrusting grip); then

2. Jab the remainder of the movement (ie. thrust your jo without any sliding).

The left/right difference is quite critical to the theory behind the jo. From the outset it should be observed that jo techniques are not to be applied ambidextrously. The right and left are employed equally, but differently. Thrusts lead with the left hand, while strikes lead with the right.

I used to think that this was a mere oddity. For a time I strenuously trained each technique equally with both hands. Or at least I tried to. No matter how hard I tried, the result was never satisfactory. Lately I've had a sort of epiphany: the right and left sides are not "unequal". They are just different. Just as the left and right hemispheres of your brain have different functions and perceive/approach the world in different ways, so your left and right hands should follow suit.

With a predominantly 2-handed weapon like the jo, your hands need to work in concert. But they must be allowed to work in their natural way. You could spend your life trying to write well with your non-preferred hand, but it would produce uncertain (and pointless) results. I have a "leftie" friend who was forced to use his right hand as a child. His handwriting (with either hand) is a disaster, and he attributes this (probably with good reason) to the forced attempts to get him to write with his right hand.

"So," I hear you ask, "where does this place left-handed jo users?" I suppose in the ideal world they would use the jo in the reverse to the "usual" manner. However because both hands are used equally (if differently) and because jo skills are not "intuitive" – they have to be learned over a lengthy period just as any fine motor skill – "lefties" don't tend to experience any real difficulty in using the jo the "standard" way. That's my experience anyway. And good thing too: it would be challenging, if not impossible, for left and right-handed students to train together using standard drills such as the kumijo.

So I'm afraid that, as with students of the katana, left-handed jo users need to accept the "injustice" of living in a right-handed world!

Details of the striking grip

I mentioned above that the right hand grip for striking is very particular. You will note from the above picture that the hand is turned over – specifically it is turned over to the point that the base knuckle of your index finger rests on the jo.

This means that the force of the strike is transmitted through your knuckle and into your hand giving your jo a solid support base. At the same time the knuckle can act to steady your jo and "guide" it along the correct path. Conversely, an "under hand" grip provides none of that "guiding" and is, moreover, weak: on heavy impact your jo is liable to slip out of your hand.

The primary stance – renoji dachi

The primary stance when using the jo is called renoji dachi – a stance that resembles the letter "L" or, more accurately, a tick (✓). The stance is formed by placing the back foot at an outward angle. In my version of the stance, the front foot is then placed on the same line as the middle of the back foot – as if your feet are resting on a balance beam. This approach is a little different from some other schools where the front foot lines up with the heel of the back foot. But the difference is deliberate and, I believe, quite crucial.

I'll explain why in a minute. The front foot is about one foot away from the line drawn by the toes of the back foot. Your weight is evenly distributed.

The "cat" stance – neko ashi dachi

The renoji dachi is almost identical to another stance used with the jo – the "cat foot" stance or neko ashi dachi. However where in the renoji dachi your weight is evenly distributed over both legs, in neko ashi dachi your back leg bears 90% of your body weight, where your front bears only 10%.

Unlike the renoji dachi, you don't place your front foot fully onto the floor: rather you place only the ball of your front foot.

Now, I mentioned above my view that it is important for the legs to be on a single line in renoji dachi (and, by extension, in neko ashi dachi). Why is that? Quite simply it is because the jo is a 2-handed weapon. With a 2-handed weapon there is an imperative for you to utilise your body as a single, harmonious unit, focusing your attention on a single line of movement. Having your body on a single line is the starting point for this emphasis.

By way of illustrating the importance of this alignment I often get my students to try a downward chopping action with the jo – first with their feet apart, then a second time with their feet in line. In every case the students report the second as feeling more powerful.

Why?

Quite simply, when you have your feet apart your attention or focus is being "split" into 2 directions. This is fine when you are unarmed or when you have a single-handed weapon. But when you have a 2-handed weapon, you need to focus your whole body behind a single movement. You literally have to pull your body into one line.

The "forward" stance – zenkutsu dachi

Another important stance used with the jo is called zenkutsu dachi, meaning "forward stance". It is principally used when you thrust your jo forwards.

The forward stance is arguably the most common stance in Eastern martial arts. In the Chinese martial arts it is known as "gong bu" while it is even seen in the hatha yoga disciplines of India where it is known as "warrior pose" – a reference to its martial connections.

The stance is formed by placing your front foot at an angle so that the outside edge points forwards. In practice this means that your foot might appear to be slightly pigeon-toed. Your back foot is angled outwards at about 30° to the front.

The distance between the outside of your feet is approximately one shoulder width while the length of the stance is approximately 2 shoulder widths.

Your front knee is bent so that your shin is vertical while your back leg is arrow-straight. This is perhaps why the stance is sometimes known as the "bow and arrow" stance.

The weight distribution in zenkutsu dachi is 70% on your front leg and 30% on your back. I often describe zenkutsu dachi as a boxer's stance, elongated and lowered. Indeed, you will often see this stance in frozen shots of a boxer executing a committed cross punch.

As with any other combat system, the zenkutsu dachi is used with the jo in the context of a lunging thrust, which is "held" only momentarily: you either withdraw from the lunge or your back leg slides up immediately into a renoji dachi.

The "open" zenkutsu dachi

A variation on the forward stance is what I call the "open zenkutsu" ("bai bu" in Chinese). In this stance, the front foot is angled so that the inside, rather than the outside, edge of your front foot points forwards. The stance is typically used in the context of evasion and preparation for counter, as you will shortly see in the suburi.

As with all stances, the open zenkutsu dachi is held temporarily. Put another way, the stances are points of transition; they are snapshots in a continuum of movement. Yes, they are sometimes assumed statically in training for the sake of conditioning. But this is an exercise only. In application they are positions of extension (eg. a lunge into the forward stance) or contraction (coiling back into cat stance).

The jodoka (jodo practitioner) will flow through these postures in a dynamic way, never pausing. A camera taking stills will however be able to pick out individual points where the stance "was held" – however fleetingly.

The "back" stance - kokutsu dachi

The kokutsu dachi – "back" stance – is used predominantly when thrusting your jo to the rear.

The stance is formed by placing the back foot at an outward angle. In this stance the front foot is then placed on the same line as the heel of the back foot approximately 2 shoulder widths away.

Unlike the renoji dachi the weight is not evenly distributed. Instead about 60% of your weight is on your "back" foot (pointing at an angle) while about 40% of your weight is on your "front" foot.

I have put "front" and "back" in quotations because you actually face backwards when you are in this stance (making what was your "front" foot your "back" foot and vice versa)!

The "horse" stance – shiko dachi

Shiko dachi – the horse stance – is another stance common to most martial arts. In Chinese it is called "mabu" (literally "horse step").

It is formed by placing your legs so that they are 2 shoulder widths apart (measuring from the heel), with your feet out at an angle.

Some schools use a horse stance where the feet point directly forward (sometimes called "kiba dachi") however I have found that the feet are best angled outward in accordance with what is comfortable for the student. The angle should however not exceed 45°.

The shiko dachi is used predominantly when attacking your opponent's knee with a low sweeping strike (gedan gaeshi). In its basic form, the shiko dachi is normally executed with a straight back, however given the flowing use of the jo, this stance occurs only in transition and accordingly a certain amount of lean is quite appropriate.

Kamae: the ready postures

There are 2 principal "ready postures" (kamae) in the art of the jo – one for use with thrusts (zuki no kamae), the other for use with strikes (uchi no kamae).

There are 2 other kamae used in katate (wrist) techniques and one used in the middle of hasso (shoulder) techniques.

Zuki no kamae

These "ready postures" are akin to the "on guard" posture in fencing or the bare-knuckle or boxing guards in unarmed fighting. Such postures provide a stable base for the launch of your techniques. In a 2-person context, they also provide the appropriate partner-to-partner signals to ensure that both parties are aware that the drill is about to commence – or alternatively that it has ended.

The latter is essential for safety in training. The jo can hurtle at great speed towards your partner. A careless move here or there could result in a broken bone or a missing eye, so great care must be taken.

The almost "ritual" nature of traditional Japanese weapons practice is sometimes ridiculed by those who don't understand its function. However these rituals give the students a time to "switch on" in terms of attaining and maintaining the state of focus necessary for combat.

The zuki no kamae

To assume the zuki no kamae, stand in a *left foot forward* renoji dachi (the primary stance) with your jo in line with your big toe and your hand holding the jo at the ¾ mark from the bottom (or, if you prefer, the ¼ mark from the top). In this posture your hand should be holding the jo with the thumb up and with a relaxed grip.

As I discussed under the subheading "The striking grip" your left and right sides are used equally in the jo – however they are not the same. The standard thrust is performed on the left. As you will see in a moment, this contrasts with the standard strike which is performed on the right. The left/right difference in these techniques is mirrored in the kamae.

The uchi no kamae

To assume the uchi no kamae, stand in a *right foot forward* renoji dachi, holding your jo with the striking grip referred to above. Your jo should be angled so that if it were extended it would touch the hollow of your opponent's throat about a metre (3 feet away from you).

Uchi no kamae

As with the zuki no kamae, your grip should be relaxed enough to permit movement, but firm enough to prevent your jo being knocked from your hands.

Take care that your right elbow is not fully straightened and that you haven't lifted your left hand excessively (pushing the tip of the jo downward into what I call the "I knight thee..." posture!).

The katate kamae

There are 2 kamae used in the case of wrist techniques, namely katate no kamae No. 1 and katate no kamae No. 2.

Katate no kamae No. 1

Katate no kamae No. 1 looks like a reverse image of the uchi no kamae.

To assume the katate no kamae No. 1, stand in a *left foot forward* renoji dachi, holding your jo with the *thrusting grip* referred to above. This kamae is used in suburi (basic technique) 11 and 12 (see pages 36 and 37).

Katate no kamae No. 2

Katate no kamae No. 2 is used only in suburi 13 (see page 38). To assume this kamae, stand in a *left foot forward* renoji dachi with your jo at your side in line with the big toe *of your back foot* and your hand holding the jo at the ¾ mark from the bottom (or, if you prefer, the ¼ mark from the top). In this posture your hand should be holding the jo with the thumb up and with a relaxed grip.

The hasso kamae

The hasso no kamae is used in suburi 13 to 18, albeit not at the start of those suburi but at the end (in the case of suburi 13), or in the middle, as a transient, preparatory posture for a strike or thrust.

To assume the kamae you will typically swing the jo up in an arc at the side of your body. As you near the top of your swing, place the butt of the jo onto your shoulder.

Hasso no kamae

Once you complete the placement of the jo on your shoulder, change your right hand grip so that your hand curves around the jo as shown in the picture below. The hasso grip change facilitates the use of the jo for striking or thrusting.

Hasso grip change

Putting it all together

As I have mentioned, there are 20 jo techniques – the suburi –, which utilise the above basic grips, stances and ready postures. To save time and space I will refer to these basics by the labels I have given them in this chapter (eg. "renoji dachi", "zuki no kamae", etc.). Please refer back to this chapter to refresh your memory as and when the need arises.

Flow: the essence of the jo

I tell my students that the essence of the jo is *flow*. The techniques must connect so that they comprise one continuous stream.

In this respect jodo is very different from arts like karate that are punctuated by abrupt staccato bursts of power. Even the flowing art of taijiquan can feature a "burst of energy" called *fajin*.

The force employed in jodo is however very different. This force is experienced in a manner similar to waves at the beach: no sooner does water crash onto the shore than it is being drawn out to sea again. The force is punctuated, but the flow is constant.

It is of course impossible for photographs to depict this constant state of motion. For that you need a live performance or the forthcoming companion DVDs.

While no book or video can be a substitute for a qualified teacher, I hope this text will serve as a guide for instructors and practitioners of the art of jodo. In particular, I hope they will find the 2-person drills a useful adjunct to understanding and applying the suburi (basics).

3. JO SUBURI: 20 TECHNIQUES

1. Choku zuki (straight thrust)

1. Start in zuki no kamae.

2. Lift your jo with your left hand while simultaneously grabbing it in the middle with your right hand, then slide your right hand down to the butt.

3. Lunge forward with your left leg into zenkutsu dachi, thrusting forward at throat height by sliding to ¼ position, then jabbing.

2. Kaeshi zuki (curved thrust)

1. Start in zuki no kamae.

2. Grab the jo with your right hand (thumb down).

3. Perform a curving deflection (kaeshi zuki – see detail on page 23), while stepping back into an open zenkutsu dachi.

4. Lunge forward with your left leg into zenkutsu dachi, thrusting forward at throat height by sliding to the ¼ position, then jabbing. (Note: your left hand is on top of the jo, palm down.)

Kaeshi zuki in detail

When executing kaeshi zuki it is important to note that it is performed by creating a circle to deflect the oncoming attack.

The angle of attack and the plane of movement in the circle are of critical importance. The circle should be performed from the floor in an arc that is about 45° to your body. Happily this circle is naturally formed by simply lifting the jo in the manner depicted in the above photographs.

The application of the kaeshi zuki is illustrated below:

Typically students will start with a larger circle and end up with a smaller, more efficient one.

When executing a kaeshi zuki, care must be taken to deflect the attack with a sliding action – not a sideways smash.

The circle of the kaeshi zuki is a subtle, but important detail that is a big part of learning to use the jo in accordance with the principle of *wu-wei* – the path of least resistance.

3. Ushiro zuki (thrust behind)

1. Start in zuki no kamae.

2. Lift jo with your right hand (thumb down) and thrust the butt forward, while bringing the jo under your left forearm. *[This movement is primarily a loading or chambering movement, however it can also be used as a strike or deflection.]*

3. Step back with your left leg into kokutsu dachi, simultaneously thrusting the jo at throat height by sliding the jo to the ¼ position, then jabbing (see detail on page 25).

Ushiro zuki in detail

In ushiro zuki, when sliding your jo to the ¼ position, you should make sure that your jo slides directly under your forearm. Only when you have reached the ¼ position should you lift the forearm away from the jo and proceed to jab. Sliding your jo underneath your forearm gives you greater control over your jo and accordingly ensures a stable and straight path for your jo thrust.

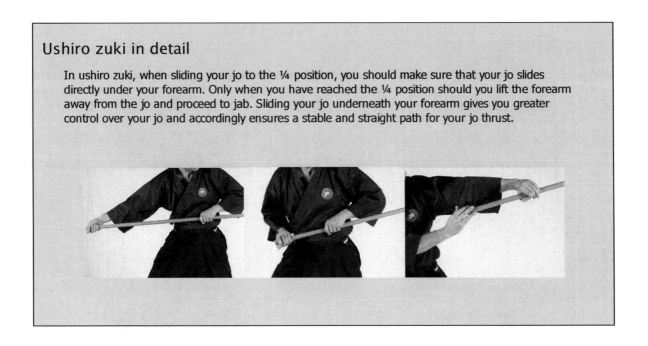

4. Zuki gedan gaeshi (thrust with a low sweeping strike)

1. Start in zuki no kamae and execute choku zuki as per suburi 1 (see page 21).

2. Once you have completed the choku zuki, begin a retreat by drawing your right leg backwards (see detail on page 27) to extend your stance.

3. Simultaneously pull the jo with your right hand to full extension.

4. Pull your left leg back into a renoji dachi.

5. Simultaneously push the jo through your right hand around your body in a clockwise direction to the ¼ position.

6. Execute a gedan gaeshi (a low sweeping attack) by moving forward with your right leg with a circular step into shiko dachi, attacking your opponent's knee.

Zuki gedan gaeshi in detail

After your thrust in zuki gedan gaeshi, make sure that your movement backwards is initiated by your *back* leg, not your front. This ensures that your body is immediately taken out of range.

If your front foot initiates the movement you will not have time to evade your opponent's thrust; you will be hit in the time it takes to shift your weight from your front foot to your back.

5. Zuki jodan gaeshi (thrust with a high curving block and strike)

1. Start in zuki no kamae and execute choku zuki as per suburi 1 (see page 21).

2. Once you have completed the choku zuki, begin a retreat by drawing your right leg backwards (see detail on page 27) to extend your stance.

3. Pull your left leg back into a neko ashi dachi.

4. Simultaneously execute a jodan sukui uke (see detail on page 29).

5. Slide your right hand down to your left and step forward with your right leg into renoji dachi, letting go of the jo with your left hand and swinging the jo around and behind your head.

6. When the butt of the jo is facing forward and your feet are parallel, grab the butt with your left hand and finish the step, executing a shomen uchi.

Jodan sukui uke in detail

The jodan sukui uke (high scooping deflection) is one of the most important techniques in jodo and it first occurs in zuki jodan gaeshi.

It is performed by drawing the hands in a vertical arc facing the opponent to an angled finishing position above the head, rear hand forward at eye height, right hand above the head and the jo angled 45° downwards and 30° away from the opponent.

I often describe this technique as inscribing a "cone" shape in the air, with the front of the jo being a few inches from the tip of the cone while the rear of the jo is at the base. This enables you to use your opponent's downward force to propel your counter.

6. Shomen uchi komi (downward strike to the front)

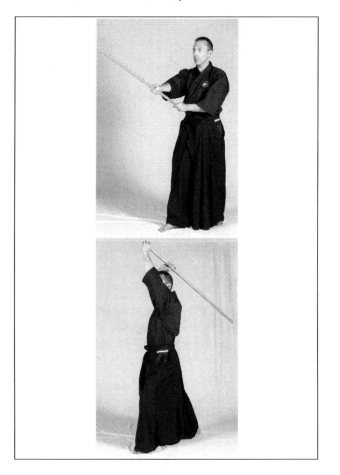 

1. Start in uchi no kamae.

2. Step back with your right leg into a left leg forward open zenkutsu dachi (see detail below), raising the jo so that it is in line with your head (looking at the opponent under your left armpit).

3. Step forward into a renoji dachi, executing a shomen uchi.

Moving back into open zenkutsu: detail

When you step back into open zenkutsu dachi, you should ensure that the toes of your back foot are *on the same line* as the outside edge of your front foot (relative to the front).

Many students step with their back leg far too much to the side. This makes it difficult to return on the counter.

Rather, if you restrict your movement to this angle, you will be able to slip the attack without over-turning.

Also take care to keep your weight on your front foot rather than shifting your weight onto your back leg (a common mistake). And don't pivot the front foot: it stays still.

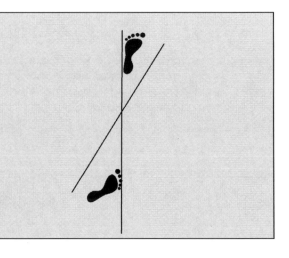

7. Renzoku uchi komi (consecutive downward strikes)

1. Start in uchi no kamae and execute shomen uchi komi as per suburi 6 (see page 30).

2. While stepping forward with your left leg, execute a jodan sukui uke (see page 29) by drawing the hands in a clockwise arc.

3. Swing your jo in a clockwise curve around your head and execute another downward strike as you step into renoji dachi.

Migi and hidari no awase – an exercise using renzoku uchi komi

This exercise is performed by starting in uchi no kamae, stepping with your back leg forward at 45° to the front and executing a jodan sukui uke. As you complete the step, it is important for your back leg to become your front leg and vice versa. The solo form is shown below:

The exercise can also be performed with a partner who is striking, or with both sides striking and deflecting.

8. Men uchi gedan gaeshi (downward strike with a low sweeping strike)

1. Start in uchi no kamae and execute shomen uchi komi as per suburi 6 (see page 30).

2. Extend the stance by drawing your left leg back, then pull your right leg back into a renoji dachi.

3. Simultaneously pull the jo with your left hand to full extension, then push the jo through your right hand around your body in an anti-clockwise direction to the ¼ position.

4. Execute a gedan gaeshi (a low sweeping attack) by moving forward with your left leg with a circular step into shiko dachi and attacking your opponent's knee.

9. Men uchi ushiro zuki (downward strike with a thrust behind)

1. Start in uchi no kamae and execute shomen uchi komi as per suburi 6 (see page 30).

2. Turn to look behind you, then slide your right hand (thumb up) to the tip of the jo.

3. Step back with your left leg into kokutsu dachi.

4. Simultaneously thrust the jo at throat height by sliding the jo (under your left forearm until your left elbow starts to straighten), to ¼ position, then jab (see detail on page 25).

10. Gyaku yoko men ushiro zuki (reverse strike to the side of the head, rear thrust)

1. Start in uchi no kamae.

2. Step forward and execute a jodan sukui uke (see detail on page 29) and follow with a gyaku yoko men uchi (reverse strike to the side of the head).

3. Slide your left hand (thumb up) to the tip of the jo.

4. Step back with your right leg into kokutsu dachi.

5. Simultaneously thrust the jo at throat height by sliding the jo (under your left forearm until your left elbow starts to straighten), to ¼ position, then jab (see detail on page 25).

11. Katate gedan gaeshi (low sweeping wrist strike)

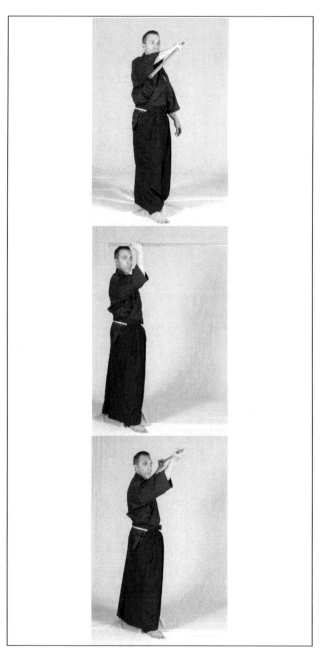

1. Start in katate no kamae No. 1.

2. Draw your right leg back, then pull your left leg back into a renoji dachi.

3. Simultaneously pull the jo to full extension, then push it behind you.

4. Step forward into renoji dachi and execute a low sweeping wrist strike to the opponent's knee, making sure your hand is palm down at the point of impact.

5. After impact, allow the jo to turn over in your wrist and catch it in a high guard.

6. Make sure you catch the jo *near your right hand, then slide your left hand down to the butt* (to facilitate catching a fast jo).

12. Toma katate uchi (extended wrist strike)

1. Start in katate no kamae No. 1.

2. Step with your back leg into kokutsu dachi and simultaneously pull your jo through your left palm while effecting a circular deflection.   Make sure your left hand remains motionless and that the jo pivots on top of your thumb and index finger.

3. Lean back and pull the jo around your head, then release the jo as a swinging long-range strike.

4. After impact, allow the jo to turn over in your wrist and catch it in a low guard at your side.

5. Make sure you catch the jo *near your right hand, then slide your left hand down to the ¼ position.*

13. Katate hachi no ji gaeshi (figure 8 sweeping wrist strike)

1. Start in katate no kamae No. 2.

2. Step forward with your right leg bringing it up next to your left while simultaneously swinging the jo from right to left in a figure 8 motion.

3. As your jo reaches the mid-point of your body, step your left leg back.

4. Keep the momentum for a return swing (the second part of the figure 8 movement). Also prepare your right arm to assist the backhand swing (which is weaker than the forehand swing because of the angle of your wrist holding the jo.

5. As your jo reaches your head height, push it down with your left hand to complete the second part of the figure 8 swing.

6. Simultaneously step forward with your left leg up to the right.

7. As your jo reaches the mid-point of your body, step your right leg back. Make it a bigger step than the previous ones.

8. Draw your left leg back into a renoji dachi and use the momentum to swing the jo over and up onto your shoulder into a hasso no kamae.

14. Hasso gaeshi uchi (shoulder sweeping strike)

1. Start in uchi no kamae.

2. Pull your jo to the ¾ position and lift the butt of your jo so that it is at face height, then place your palm against the jo to help propel it into a swing.

3. Take a big step back with your right leg, then draw your left leg back into renoji dachi.

4. Simultaneously push down on your jo with your left hand, propelling it into a swing at the side of your body.

5. Use the momentum to swing the jo over and up onto your shoulder into a hasso no kamae.

15. Hasso gaeshi zuki (shoulder sweeping thrust)

6. Lift your jo off your shoulder and raise it above your head. Load the jo by cocking back your wrists so that the jo falls behind your head.

7. Step forward into renoji dachi and execute shomen uchi.

1. Start in uchi no kamae.

2. Pull your jo to the ¾ position and lift the butt of your jo so that it is at face height.

3. Take a big step back with your right leg, then draw your left leg back into renoji dachi.

4. Simultaneously push down on your jo with your left hand, propelling it into a swing at the side of your body.

5. Use the momentum to swing the jo over and up onto your shoulder into a hasso no kamae.

6. Use your left hand to pull your jo through your right to full extension.

7. Lunge forward with your left leg into kokutsu dachi.

8. Simultaneously slide your jo to the ¼ position, then jab.

9. If you want, you can slide up your right leg into a renoji dachi as you effect your thrust, or you can stay in kokutsu dachi.

16. Hasso gaeshi ushiro zuki (shoulder sweeping reverse thrust)

1. Start in uchi no kamae.

2. Pull your jo to the ¾ position and lift the butt of your jo so that it is at face height, then place your palm against the jo to help propel it into a swing.

3. Take a big step back with your right leg, then draw your left leg back into renoji dachi.

4. Simultaneously push down on your jo with your left hand, propelling it into a swing at the side of your body.

5. Use the momentum to swing the jo over and up onto your shoulder into a hasso no kamae.

6. After changing the grip on your right hand (see page 17) slide your left hand up to the ¾ position, then step back into kokutsu dachi.

7. Simultaneously effect an ushiro zuki (see detail on page 25).

17. Hasso gaeshi ushiro uchi (shoulder sweeping reverse strike)

1. Start in uchi no kamae.

2. Pull your jo to the ¾ position and lift the butt of your jo so that it is at face height, then place your palm against the jo to help propel it into a swing.

3. Take a big step back with your right leg, then draw your left leg back into renoji dachi.

4. Simultaneously push down on your jo with your left hand, propelling it into a swing at the side of your body.

5. Use the momentum to swing the jo over and up onto your shoulder into a hasso no kamae.

18. Hasso gaeshi ushiro harai
(shoulder sweeping reverse circular strike)

6. Pivot on the balls of both feet so as to turn to the rear, simultaneously executing a strike to the side of your opponent's knee.

1. Start in uchi no kamae.

2. Pull your jo to the ¾ position and lift the butt of your jo so that it is at face height, then place your palm against the jo to help propel it into a swing.

3. Take a big step back with your right leg, then draw your left leg back into renoji dachi.

4. Simultaneously push down on your jo with your left hand, propelling it into a swing at the side of your body. Use the momentum to swing the jo over and up onto your shoulder into a hasso no kamae.

5. Pivot on the ball of your left foot so as to turn to the rear, simultaneously swinging your jo around your head for a cutting strike.

19. Hidari nagare gaeshi uchi (left flowing and sweeping strike)

6. As you complete your turn to the rear, pull your right leg back in an arc and execute the lateral strike at approximately mid-body level.

7. After you've complete your strike allow your hands to turn over and the jo to come to a rest in a low side guard.

1. Start in uchi no kamae.

2. Execute shomen uchi komi as per suburi 6 (see page 30).

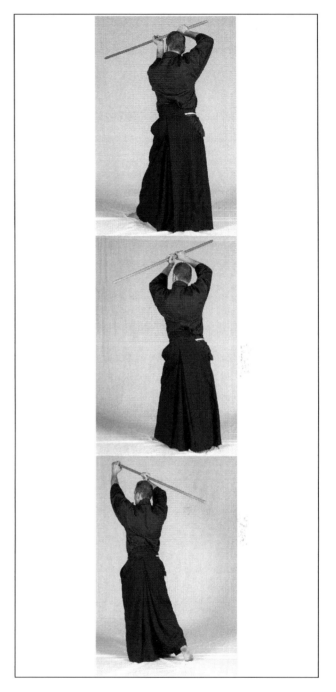

3. Let go of the jo with your left hand and tilt the jo to the left, then grab it again with your left hand near the middle of the jo.

4. Pivot on the toes of both feet and turn 180°, executing a jodan sukui uke (see detail on page 29).

5. Slide your left hand to your right, allow the jo to swing around and grab the butt with your left hand.

6. Load the jo by cocking back your wrists so that the jo falls behind your head.

7. Step forward with your right leg and execute a shomen uchi.

8. Pivot on the toes of both feet and turn 180°.

9. Repeat moves 3 and 4.

10. Repeat moves 5, 6 and 7.

11. From here you can stop, or keep repeating the sequence.

20. Migi nagare gaeshi zuki (right flowing and sweeping thrust)

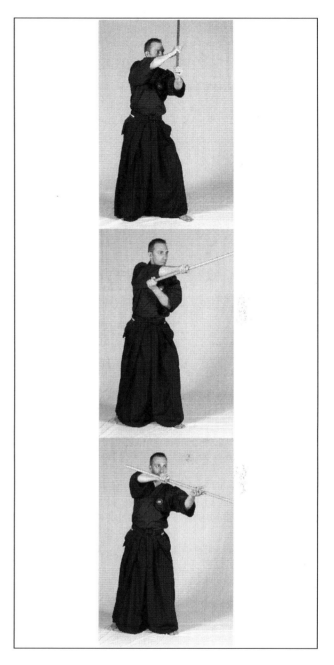

1. Start in uchi no kamae.

2. Step forward and execute a jodan sukui uke (see detail on page 29).

3. Follow with a gyaku yoko men uchi (reverse strike to the side of the head – see page 35).

4. Let go of the jo with your left hand and tilt the jo to the right, then grab it again with your left hand near the middle of the jo.

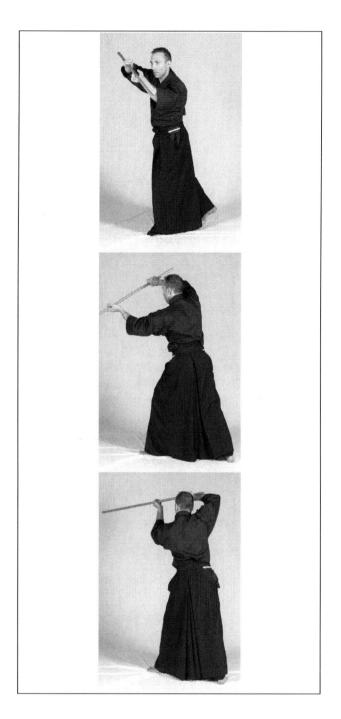

5. Pivot on the toes of your left foot and turn 180°, swinging your right leg around in an arc.

6. Simultaneous execute a gyaku jodan sukui uke (ie. a brushing movement from left to right at head height).

7. Lower the jo into the thrusting grip (see page 10) and step forward into zenkutsu dachi.

8. Simultaneously execute a choku zuki (see page 21).

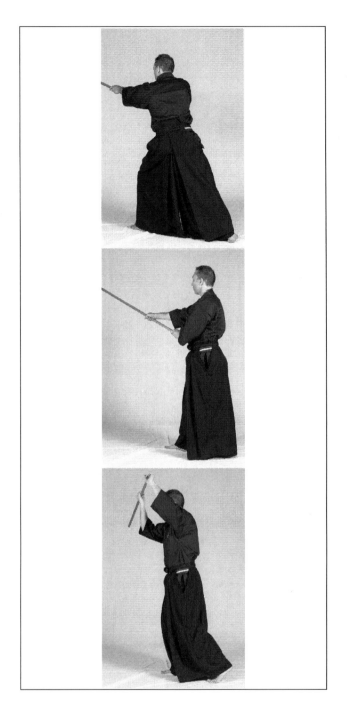

9. After you complete the choku zuki, step forward with your right leg into renoji dachi and adjust your grip so that you are in uchi no kamae.

10. Repeat move 2.

11. Repeat move 3.

12. Repeat moves 3, 5 and 6.

13. Repeat moves 7 and 8.

14. From here you can stop, or keep repeating the sequence.

4. KUMIJO: 2-PERSON DRILLS

Kumijo 1 (using suburi 1, 2 and 4)

Single person performance of kumijo 1

1. Start in zuki no kamae. Execute a kaeshi uke (the first part of suburi 2 – see page 23).

2. Execute a kaeshi zuki (the second part of suburi 2 – see page 22).

3. Draw your right leg back and the pull your left leg up against your right shin, stabbing your jo into the ground.

The drill is now at its half-way point. In a 2-person performance, the other side starts at move 4.

4. Drop your foot and lunge forward executing a choku zuki (suburi 1 – see page 21).

5. Execute a gedan gaeshi evasion (the second part of suburi 4 – see page 26).

6. Execute a gedan gaeshi (the third part of suburi 4 – see page 26). After you complete the strike, slide your left hand down to your right.

The drill is now back to its beginning. You can choose to continue cycling through the drill or stop. To continue, proceed to move 7 (ie. move 1) below:

7. Grab the top of the jo with your right hand, step back into renoji dachi, then execute a kaeshi uke (ie. you are back to move 1 of this drill).

Side A begins with move 1 (the kaeshi uke in defence against side B who begins with move 4 (choku zuki).

Side A counters with move 2 (kaeshi zuki) while side B evades using move 5 (the gedan gaeshi evasion).

Side A then evades and blocks using move 3, in defence against side B who attacks with move 6 (a gedan gaeshi).

The drill is now at its half-way point. From here the sides will swap roles.

Side A counters with move 4 (choku zuki) which side B evades and deflects using move 7 or 1 (the kaeshi uke).

Side A evades using move 5 (the gedan gaeshi evasion) in defence against side B who attacks with move 2 (kaeshi zuki).

Side A then attacks with move 6 (a gedan gaeshi) while side A evades and blocks using move 3.

The drill is now back to its beginning. The sides can choose to continue cycling through the drill or stop.

Side B evades and deflects using move 7 or 1 (kaeshi uke) against side A who attacks with move 4 (choku zuki).

Kumijo 2 (using suburi 2, 5, 6 and 7)

Single person performance of kumijo 2

1. Start in katate no kamae No. 1. Draw back into neko ashi dachi and execute a jodan sukui uke (the second part of suburi 5 – see page 28).

2. Step forwards with your right leg into renoji dachi and execute a shomen uchi.

3. While stepping forward with your left leg, execute a jodan sukui uke (see detail on page 29) by drawing the hands in a vertical clockwise arc.

4. Pivot on your left toes to turn 180°, swinging your right foot around in an arc.

5. Simultaneously swing your jo in a clockwise curve around your head and execute a downward strike to your opponent's knee.

6. Let go of the jo with your left hand, then grab it again near the middle of the jo.

7. Slide your right hand down to the butt and execute a kaeshi uke (the first part of suburi 1 – see page 22).

The drill is now at its half-way point. In a 2-person performance, the other side starts at move 8.

8. Execute a kaeshi zuki (the second part of suburi 1 – see page 22).

9. Draw back into neko ashi dachi and execute a jodan sukui uke (the second part of suburi 5 – see page 28) but this time with both hands gripping the jo palm down.

10. As you execute the jodan sukui uke, slide your right hand to your left.

11. Step forward and execute a shomen uchi.

12. Take another step forward while simultaneously tilting your jo clockwise and dropping it to the side and behind you so as to deflect a low attack to your right knee.

13. Pivot on your right toes to turn 180°, swinging your right foot around in an arc.

14. Simultaneously swing the jo around your head in a clockwise arc, executing a reverse downward strike (the second part of suburi 7 – see page 31).

The drill is now back to its beginning. You can choose to continue cycling through the drill or stop.   To continue, proceed to move 15 (ie. move 1) below:

15. Let go of the jo with your left hand, then grab it again near the middle of the jo, draw back into neko ashi dachi and execute a jodan sukui uke. (ie. you are back to move 1 of this drill).

2-person performance of kumijo 2

Side A begins with move 7 (the kaeshi uke) in defence against side B who begins with move 14 (the renzoku uchi komi).

Side A counters with move 8 (kaeshi zuki) while side B evades using move 1 (the gedan gaeshi evasion).

This is actually the start of the single person drill.

Side A then evades and blocks using move 9, in defence against side B who attacks with move 2 (a downward strike).

Side A counters with move 10 (a downward strike) while side B while side B steps forward and deflects the strike using move 3 (jodan sukui uke).

Side A then evades and blocks using move 12 in defence against side B who attacks with move 5 (a low strike to the knee). Side A then counters with move 14 (reverse downward strike).

Side B counters the downward strike by using move 7 (kaeshi uke). **The drill is now at its halfway point.** From here the sides will swap roles.

Side A then evades and blocks using move 1 (jodan sukui uke) in defence against side B who attacks with move 8 (kaeshi zuki).

Side A then attacks with move 2 (a downward strike) which side B evades and blocks using move 9.

Side A steps forward and effects move 3 (jodan sukui uke) in defence against side B who attacks with move 10 (a downward strike). Side A then prepares for a downward strike.

Kumijo 3 (using suburi 3, 5 and 8)

Single person performance of kumijo 3

Side A then attacks with move 5 (a strike to the knee) which B evades and blocks using move 12. Side A then counters with move 14.

Side A then effects move 7 (kaeshi uke) in defence against side B who attacks with move 14 (reverse downward strike).

The drill is back to its beginning.

1. Start in zuki no kamae. Lift the jo and perform the first movement of suburi 3 (see page 24). In this case the move is used as a deflection of an incoming thrust. *[This technique is particularly useful against a surprise attack.]*

2. Lunge forward with your left leg and turn your body so that you assume a kokutsu dachi.

3. Simultaneously inscribe a clockwise circle with the tip of your jo towards the front (kake uke). This move is used to hook the attacking jo around and into the ground.

4. Having completed the downward parry, lift your jo and effect an ushiro zuki (see pages 24 and 25).

5. After you have completed your thrust, pull the jo through your left hand with your right until the jo is at full extension.

6. Position your jo on your right hand so that it is resting along the inside of your lowest knuckle of your index finger. You will exert pressure on this knuckle as you perform a downward strike in the next move.

7. Step back with your left leg into renoji dachi and slide your right hand down to the ¼ position, effecting a shomen uchi.

8. While holding your jo in uchi no kamae, execute a *quick jab*. [*This is the only instance of thrusting from uchi no kamae.*]

9. Draw the jo to full extension and step back with your right leg into renoji dachi, executing a low block past your left knee. [*This is a more linear movement than gedan gaeshi.*]

10. Let go of the jo with your right hand and grab it again at the other end.

The drill is now at its halfway point. In a 2-person performance, the other side starts at move 10.

11. Lunge forward into zenkutsu dachi and execute choku zuki (see page 21).

12. Draw back into neko ashi dachi and execute the jodan sukui uke (the first part of suburi 5 – see page 28).

13. Step forward into renoji dachi and execute a shomen uchi (the second part of suburi 5 – see page 28).

14. Execute the second part of suburi 8 (an evasion).

15. Follow this with a gedan gaeshi (low sweeping strike – see page 33).

2-person performance of kumijo 3

The drill is now back to its beginning. You can choose to continue cycling through the drill or stop. To continue, proceed to move 15 (ie. move 1) below:

16. Lift the jo and perform the first movement of suburi 3 (see page 24).

Side A begins with move 1 (the first movement of suburi 3) in defence against side B who begins with move 10 (choku zuki).

Side A counters with moves 2 and 3 (kake uke).

After executing the kake uke, side A continues with move 4 (ushiro zuki) which side B deflects using move 11 (jodan sukui uke).

Side A then executes move 6 (shomen uchi) in defence against side B who attacks with move 12 (also shomen uchi). Side A's shomen uchi would, in reality, strike side B's right hand, but in practice the strike lands on the jo.

Side A then executes move 7 (a jab) which side B counters with move 13 (a gedan gaeshi evasion).

Side A executes move 8 (a low block) in defence against side B who attacks using move 14 (gedan gaeshi).

The drill is now at its halfway point. From here the sides will swap roles.

Side A begins with move 10 (choku zuki) which side B deflects using move 1 (the first movement of suburi 3).

Side B counters with moves 2 and 3 (kake uke).

After executing the kake uke, side B continues with move 4 (ushiro zuki) which side A deflects using move 11 (jodan sukui uke).

Side A then executes move 12 (shomen uchi) which side B counters using move 6 (also shomen uchi).

Side A executes move 13 (a gedan gaeshi evasion) in defence against side B who attacks with move 7 (a jab).

Side A attacks using move 14 (gedan gaeshi) which side B counters using move 8 (a low block).

Kumijo 4 (using suburi 9 and 10)

Single person performance of kumijo 4

The drill is now back to its beginning. The sides can choose to continue cycling through the drill or stop.

1. Start in uchi no kamae. Pull the jo through your right hand to full extension, tilt the jo to the left and step back with your right leg into kokutsu dachi and effect a vertical sweeping block to your right side.

2. Lift the jo to horizontal and effect an ushiro zuki.

3. Pull the jo through your left hand to full extension.

4. Position your jo on your right hand so that it is resting along the inside of your lowest knuckle of your index finger. You will exert pressure on this knuckle as you perform a downward strike in the next move.

5. Step back with your left leg into renoji dachi executing a shomen uchi.

6. After executing shomen uchi, step forward and execute a sukui uke.

The drill is now at its halfway point. In a 2-person performance, the other side starts at move 5.

7. Execute a gyaku yoko men uchi.

8. Let go of the jo with your left hand and grab it near the middle, tilting the tip of the jo down as you do so.

9. Step back with your right leg into kokutsu dachi and effect a vertical sweeping block to your left side.

10. Lift the jo to horizontal and effect an ushiro zuki.

2-person performance of kumijo 4

11. Slide the right hand up to the left (this is important to avoid getting your hand hit), then grab the butt with your right hand and lunge forward with your right leg, effecting a shomen uchi.

The drill is now back to its beginning. You can choose to continue cycling through the drill or stop. To continue, proceed to move 1.

Side A begins with move 1 (hikkake uke) in defence against side B who begins with move 5 (gyaku yoko men uchi).

Side A responds with move 2 (ushiro zuki) which side B deflects with move 7 (hikkake uke).

Side B then loads the jo for an ushiro zuki.

Side A steps back and executes move 3 (shomen uchi) in defence against side B who attacks with move 8 (ushiro zuki). Side A then uses move 4 (jodan sukui uke) in defence against side B who attacks with move 9 (shomen uchi).

The drill is now at its halfway point. From here the sides will swap roles.

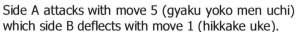

Side A attacks with move 5 (gyaku yoko men uchi) which side B deflects with move 1 (hikkake uke).

Side A then uses move 7 (hikkake uke) in defence against side B who counters with move 2 (ushiro zuki).

Side A then attacks with move 8 (ushiro zuki) which side B deflects by stepping back and executing move 3 (shomen uchi).

Side A attacks with move 9 (shomen uchi) which side B deflects using move 4 (jodan sukui uke).

The drill is now back to its beginning. The sides can choose to continue cycling through the drill or stop.

Side A begins with move 1 in defence against side B who begins with move 5.

Kumijo 5 (using suburi 11 and 15)

Single person performance of kumijo 5

1. Start in katate kamae No. 1 and execute the first part of suburi 11 (see page 36) which involves a downward deflection, loading your jo behind you.

2. Execute the katate gedan gaeshi and catch
    your jo in the high guard.

As discussed in relation to suburi 11, it is important
not to turn over the hand until after the point of
impact. At the point of impact the middle knuckles
of your hand holding the jo should point in the
direction of the strike.

3. After you complete suburi 11, effect
    suburi 15 (see page 41). To do this, pull
    the jo to the ¾ position, place your left
    palm near the middle of the jo and
    execute the hasso gaeshi uke on your right
    side.

4. Complete the hasso gaeshi uke and place the jo on your shoulder in the hasso no kamae.

It is important to remember that the hasso gaeshi uke is a powerful deflection, similar to the kaeshi uke. Remember also to effect the hasso grip change as shown on page 17.

The drill is now at its halfway point. In a 2-person performance, the other side starts at move 5.

5. Pull the jo through your right hand, then lunge forward with your left leg and effect a high thrust.

6. Let go of the jo with your right hand and let it flip, catching it again with your right at what was the tip of the jo (but is now the butt.

7. Extend your stance by stepping back with your right (back) leg (see detail on page 27).

8. Draw up your left leg into neko ashi dachi at 30° to the left of the front.

9. Simultaneously execute a hikkake uke deflection/block on your left.

10. Pull your jo through your right hand to full extension, lunge forward with your right leg into renoji dachi and execute a high thrust.

2-person performance of kumijo 5

The drill is now back to its beginning. You can choose to continue cycling through the drill or stop. To continue, proceed to move 8 (ie. move 1) below:

    11. Execute suburi 11 (see page 36) – ie. a wrist strike to your opponent's knee.

Side A begins with move 1, utilizing the downward motion as a deflection in defence against side B who begins with move 5 (a high thrust).

Side A continues with move 2 (katate gedan gaeshi) which side B blocks using move 7 (hikkake uke).

Side A swings the jo around to effect move 3 (hasso gaeshi uke) which he uses in defence against side B who attacks with move 8 (a high thrust).

Side A continues to move 4 (assuming the hasso no kamae) while side B prepares for move 1 (a downward deflection, loading your jo behind you).

The drill is now at its halfway point. From here the sides will swap roles.

Side A effects move 5 (a high thrust) which side B deflects using move 1 (a downward deflection).

Side A uses move 7 (hikkake uke) in defence against side B who uses move 2 (katate gedan gaeshi).

Side A attacks with move 8 (a high thrust) which side B deflects using move 3 (hasso gaeshi uke).

Kumijo 6 (using suburi 1 and 12)

Single person performance of kumijo 6

The drill is now back to its beginning. The sides can choose to continue cycling through the drill or stop.

Side A uses move 1 (a downward deflection) in defence against side B who effects move 5 (a high thrust).

1. Start in katate no kamae No. 1 and execute the first part of suburi 12 (see page 37) which involves a curving overhead deflection.

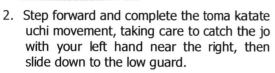

2. Step forward and complete the toma katate uchi movement, taking care to catch the jo with your left hand near the right, then slide down to the low guard.

3. Step back, simultaneously sliding your left hand up the jo as you bring it from your left so that the tip points at your opponent. This movement is used as a pressing (osae) deflection.

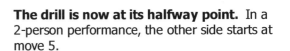

4. Lunge forward with your left leg and execute a choku zuki.

The drill is now at its halfway point. In a 2-person performance, the other side starts at move 5.

5. Let go of the jo with your right hand, flip it over and grab it again at the other end and execute a high thrust. The flip over is useful both to execute quick successive thrusts and also to "go with the flow" when your jo is knocked out of the grasp of one hand (ie. it is consistent with the principle of "wu-wei").

6. Let go of the jo with your right hand and let it flip, catching it again with your right at what was the tip of the jo.

7. Extend your stance by stepping back with your right (back) leg (see detail on page 27).

8. Draw up your left leg into neko ashi dachi at 30° to the left of the front. Simultaneously execute a hikkake uke on your left.

9. Pull your jo through your right hand to full extension, lunge forward with your right leg into renoji dachi and execute a high thrust.

2-person performance of kumijo 6

10. Pull the jo through your left hand to full extension then step back with your right leg into renoji dachi executing a reverse shomen uchi. *[This is one of only two instances where downward striking occurs on the left.]*

The drill is now back to its beginning. You can choose to continue cycling through the drill or stop. To continue, proceed to move 1.

Side A begins with move 1 (overhead deflection) in defence against side B who begins with move 5 (a high thrust).

Side A continues with move 2 (toma katate uchi) which side B blocks using move 7 (hikkake uke).

Side A uses move 3 (osae uke) in defence against side B who attacks with move 8 (a high thrust).

Side A counters with move 4 (choku zuki) which side B deflects using move 9 (a reverse shomen uchi). **The drill is now at its halfway point.** From here the sides will swap roles.

Side A attacks with move 5 (a high thrust) which side B deflects with move 1 (overhead deflection).

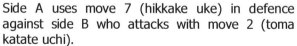

Side A uses move 7 (hikkake uke) in defence against side B who attacks with move 2 (toma katate uchi).

Side A uses move 3 (osae uke) in defence against side B who attacks with move 8 (a high thrust).

Side A attacks with move 8 (a high thrust) which side B deflects using move 3 (osae uke).

Side A uses move 9 (a reverse shomen uchi) in defence against side B who attacks with move 4 (choku zuki).

Kumijo 7 (using suburi 1, 5, 13, 14 and 15)

Single person performance of kumijo 7

The drill is now back to its beginning. The sides can choose to continue cycling through the drill or stop.

Side A uses move 1 (overhead deflection) in defence against side B who attacks with move 5 (a high thrust), etc.

1. Start in katate no kamae No. 2. Draw back into neko ashi dachi and execute a jodan sukui uke.

2. Instead of continuing with a shomen uke (eg. the second part of suburi 5 – see page 28), circle your jo back along the same plane in an anti-clockwise direction and load the jo for a thrust.

3. Lunge forward into zenkutsu dachi and execute a choku zuki.

4. After you complete your thrust, pull the jo through your left hand to the ¾ position.

5. Execute a hachi no ji (figure 8) deflection to the left (as per suburi 13 – see page 38) as your step back with your left leg into renoji dachi.

6. Continue with a hasso gaeshi uke on your right side as per suburi 13, making sure you use your palm to push down on the jo and propel it into the spin.

7. Complete the hasso gaeshi uke to assume the hasso no kamae.

The drill is now at its halfway point. In a 2-person performance, the other side starts at move 8.

8. Load the jo above your head for a shomen uchi.

9. Step forward with your right leg and execute a shomen uchi (as per suburi 14 – see page 40).

10. Pull the jo through your right hand to the ¾ position.

11. Execute another hasso gaeshi uke on your right side.

12. Complete the hasso gaeshi uke to assume a hasso no kamae, then lunge forward with the left foot, pulling the jo through the left hand to full extension.

13. Execute a high thrust as per suburi 15 (see page 41).

14. Let go of the jo with your right hand, flip it over and grab it again at the other end and execute a high thrust. The flip over is useful both to execute quick successive thrusts and also to "go with the flow" when your jo is knocked out of the grasp of one hand (ie. it is consistent with the principle of "wu-wei").

[For the reverse flip, see kumijo 6 on page 97.]

The drill is now back to its beginning. You can choose to continue cycling through the drill or stop. To continue, proceed to move 15 (ie. move 1) below:

15. Draw back into neko ashi dachi and execute a jodan sukui uke.

2-person performance of kumijo 7

Side A begins with move 1 (jodan sukui uke) in defence against side B who begins with move 8 (shomen uchi).

Side A counters with move 3 (choku zuki) which side B deflects using move 11 (hasso gaeshi uke).

Side A uses moves 5 and 6 (hachi no ji gaeshi and hasso gaeshi) in defence against side B who attacks with moves 13 and 14 (2 consecutive thrusts).

[Note that the impact of the hachi no ji gaeshi will naturally lend side B to flip the jo in the consecutive thrusts.]

The drill is now at its halfway point. From here the sides will swap roles.

Side A counters with move 9 (shomen uchi) which side B deflects using move 1 (jodan sukui uke).

Side A uses move 11 (hasso gaeshi uke) in defence against side B who attacks with move 3 (choku zuki).

Side A attacks with moves 13 and 14 (2 consecutive thrusts) while side B deflects them with moves 5 and 6 (hachi no ji gaeshi and hasso gaeshi).

[Note that the impact of the hachi no ji gaeshi will naturally lend side A to flip the jo in the consecutive thrusts.]

The drill is now back to its beginning. The sides can choose to continue cycling through the drill or stop.

Side A uses move 1 (jodan sukui uke) in defence against side B who attacks with move 8 (shomen uchi), etc.

Kumijo 8 (using suburi 5, 14 and 16)

Single person performance of kumijo 8

1. Start in uchi no kamae. Pull the jo to the ¾ position and raise the jo in preparation for a hasso gaeshi uke.

2. Step back with your left leg and execute a hasso gaeshi uke on your right side.

3. After you have assumed a hasso no kamae, let go of the jo with your left hand and lower the jo with your right.

4. As you lower the jo, slide your left hand (formerly at the base), slide it up to the top and grab it again.

5. Step back with your left leg into renoji dachi and simultaneously execute a hikkake uke.

6. Lunge forward with your right leg into kokutsu dachi and execute an ushiro zuki.

7. Pull the jo through your left hand to full extension then step back with your right leg into renoji dachi executing a reverse shomen uchi. *[This is the second of only 2 instances where downward striking occurs on the left.]*

The drill is now at its halfway point. In a 2-person performance, the other side starts at move 7.

8. Lunge forward with the left leg into zenkutsu dachi and execute a choku zuki.

11. Let go of the jo with your right hand, flip it over and grab it again at the other end.

The flip over is useful both to execute quick successive thrusts and also to "go with the flow" when your jo is knocked out of the grasp of one hand (ie. it is consistent with the principle of "wu-wei").

[For the reverse flip, see kumijo 7 on page 108.]

9. Execute a high thrust.

10. As you complete your thrust, change your right hand grip to allow you to execute a jodan gaeshi uke.

11. Execute a jodan gaeshi uke.

12. Step through and execute a shomen uchi as per suburi 5 (see page 29).

The drill is now back to its beginning. You can choose to continue cycling through the drill or stop.

Side A begins with move 1 (hasso gaeshi uke) in defence against side B who begins with move 7 (choku zuki).

[Note that the impact of the hasso gaeshi uke will naturally lend side B to flip the jo.]

Side A uses move 4 (hikkake uke) in defence against side B who has flipped his jo and is attacking with move 8 (a high thrust).

Side A attacks using move 5 (ushiro zuki or high thrust) which side B counters with move 10 (jodan sukui uke).

Side A starts stepping back and loads his jo while side B loads his jo for a shomen uchi.

Side A uses move 6 (reverse shomen uchi) in defence against side B who attacks with move 11 (shomen uchi).

The drill is now at its halfway point. From here the sides will swap roles.

Side A attacks with move 7 (choku zuki) which side B counters with move 1 (hasso gaeshi uke).

Side A flips his jo and attacks with move 8 (a high thrust) which side B deflects using move 4 (hikkake uke).

[Note that the impact of the hasso gaeshi uke will naturally lend side B to flip the jo.]

Side A uses move 10 (jodan sukui uke) in defence against side B who attacks with move 5 (ushiro zuki or high thrust).

Side A attacks with move 11 (shomen uchi) which side B deflects using move 6 (rev. shomen uchi).

The drill is now back to its beginning.

Kumijo 9 (using suburi 19 and 20)

Single person performance of kumijo 9

You can choose to continue cycling through the drill or stop. To continue, Side A uses move 1 (hasso gaeshi uke) in defence against side B who attacks with move 7 (choku zuki), etc.

1. Start in uchi no kamae. Step forward with your left leg into renoji dachi and execute a jodan sukui uke.

2. Execute a gyaku yoko men uchi.

3. As you complete the strike, let go of the jo with your left hand and grab it again near the middle.

4. Slide your right hand down to the butt, pivot on your left toes and turn 180°, effecting a gyaku jodan sukui uke.

5. Pivot on your left toes approximately 45° to the left, executing a standard jodan sukui uke. As you complete the deflection, slide your right hand down to your left.

6. Step forward with your right leg into renoji dachi and execute a shomen uchi.

7. Step forward with your left leg and execute a jodan sukui uke. *[Note, this jodan sukui uke is not used in the 2 person drill except to "wind up" for the next strike.]* **The drill is now at its halfway point.** In a 2-person performance, the other side starts at move 8.

8. Follow with a gyaku yoko men uchi.

9. Let go of the jo with your left hand and grab it again near the middle. Slide your right hand down to the butt and begin pivoting on your left toes.

10. Pivot 180º, effecting a gyaku jodan sukui uke.

11. Lunge forward with your left leg into zenkutsu dachi and effect a choku zuki.

12. Let go of the jo with your right hand, flip it over and grab it again at the other end.

The flip over is useful both to execute quick successive thrusts and also to "go with the flow" when your jo is knocked out of the grasp of one hand (ie. it is consistent with the principle of "wu-wei").

[For the reverse flip, see kumijo 7 on page 108.]

13. Execute a high thrust.

14. Pull the jo through your left hand to full extension, step back with your left leg into renoji dachi and execute a shomen uchi.

The drill is now back to its beginning. You can choose to continue cycling through the drill or stop.

2-person performance of kumijo 9

Side A attacks with move 8 (gyaku yoko men uchi) which side B deflects using move 1 (jodan sukui uke)

Side A then uses move 10 (gyaku jodan sukui uke) in defence against side B who attacks with move 2 (gyaku yoko men uchi).

Side A attacks with move 11 (choku zuki) which side B deflects with move 4 (gyaku jodan sukui uke).

Side A then attacks with move 13 (high thrust) which side B deflects with move 5 (jodan sukui uke).

Side A uses move 14 (shomen uchi) in defence against side B who attacks with move 6 (shomen uchi). **The drill is now at its halfway point.**

Side A uses move 1 (jodan sukui uke) in defence against side B who attacks with move 8 (gyaku yoko men uchi).

Side A then attacks with move 2 (gyaku yoko men uchi) which side B deflects using move 10 (gyaku jodan sukui uke).

Side A uses move 4 (gyaku jodan sukui uke) in defence against side B who attacks with move 11 (choku zuki).

The drill is now back to its beginning.

The sides can choose to continue cycling through the drill or stop.

Side A then uses move 5 (jodan sukui uke) in defence against side B who attacks with move 13 (high thrust).

Side A attacks with move 6 (shomen uchi) which side B deflects using move 14 (shomen uchi).

5. AFTERWORDS

Acknowledgements

I would like to thank my senior student Jeff Cosgrove for his assistance in preparing this text – not only for posing for approximately 900 photographs, but also for the many early morning training sessions in preparation for the photo sessions.

Jeff is a 4th dan who has been training with me since 1987. He is a supremely gifted martial artist and an instructor at the Academy of Traditional Fighting Arts in Perth, Australia.

In addition to studying under me, Jeff has also trained directly under my first instructor Bob Davies.

I would like to thank my student and cousin Branko Mijatovic for posing with me in the studio photographs and assisting generally in the photography.

Branko is a green belt at the Academy of Traditional Fighting Arts in Perth, Australia, having previously trained in the shotokan system of karate-do.

I would like to thank our principal photographer Lucia Ondrusova for the many hours of her professional assistance, both in taking over 1200 photographs and editing them.

Lucia is based in Melbourne, Australia and regularly undertakes martial arts photography assignments, particularly for my Chen Pan Ling senior James Sumarac and our teacher Chen Yun Ching. She can be contacted via her website at www.luciaondrusova.com.

I would like to thank my brother Nenad Djurdjevic – the Principal of the Academy of Traditional Fighting Arts (see www.tfaperth.com) and the proprietor of the Bayswater Martial Arts and Yoga Centre (see www.martialartsandyoga.com). Apart from being an accomplished martial artist with a background corresponding to my own, Nenad is also an experienced yoga practitioner and teacher who holds degrees in both mechanical engineering and sports science and a diploma in education.

Nenad not only gave us free use of his centre for the various photo shoots, but personally took over 400 of the paired photographs.

Last, but not least, I would like to thank my martial colleague and friend Jeff Mann for his kind assistance in proof-reading and editing this text.

About the author

Dejan (Dan) Djurdjevic commenced his martial arts training in February 1981 in Durban, South Africa under the tutelage of the respected traditional martial arts teacher and researcher, Bob Davies.

Over the next 16 years Dan's studies encompassed goju-ryu karatedo, aikido (including aikijo), Okinawan kobudo, wing chun and Filipino arnis.

From 1990 he began studying the Tang Shao Dao system, as taught to Bob Davies by the late Chinese internal arts master Hong Yi Xiang of Taibei, Taiwan. This system principally comprised the arts of xingyiquan, baguazhang and taijiquan, with some precursor external (Shaolin) forms.

Under Bob Davies, Dan also began studying the Tenshin Shoden Katori Shinto Ryu system of katana and jo during 1996.

In 2005 Dan became a student of Chen Yun Ching of Taijung, Taiwan. Chen Yun Ching is the son of the late Chen Pan Ling, arguably one of the 20th century's foremost authorities on the internal arts (Chen Pan Ling was Hong Yi Xiang's instructor). Grandmaster Chen Yun Ching is the heir to the Chen Pan Ling martial system.

In January 2009 Dan was accepted as a *bai shi* (inner circle student) of the Chen Yun Ching in a ceremony in Taiwan. In his capacity as a bai shi, Dan shares the honour and responsibility of preserving and disseminating the Chen Pan Ling martial system.

Dan is presently the chief instructor of the Academy of Traditional Fighting Arts which he co-founded with his brother Nenad in April, 1985 (see www.traditionalfightingarts.com). The Academy's headquarters is located at the Bayswater Martial Arts and Yoga Centre in Perth, Australia (see www.martialartsandyoga.com). It is there that Dan teaches classes in karate, jodo, arnis and the Chen Pan Ling system.

Apart from martial instruction, Dan is also the author of the award-winning martial arts blog "The Way of Least Resistance" (www.dandjurdjevic.blogspot.com) and the founder and administrator of the Traditional Fighting Arts Forums (www.tfaforum.com).

This online activity reflects Dan's lifelong interest in researching martial technique, history and philosophy. In particular Dan enjoys cross-referencing Okinawan karate and the Chinese martial tradition.

Dan is currently working on his next martial arts text, "Applied Karate". He hopes to write a follow up to this book, titled "Advanced Jo" and to release a series of companion DVDs for both jo books.

Dan is also the author of the novel "The Mirror Image of Sound". His second work of fiction, the novella "Hazy Shade of Twilight", is due to be published in early 2015.

Dan lives in Perth, Western Australia. He is married and has 2 children.

APPENDIX: MUIDOKAN JO SYLLABUS

Note: The Muidokan jodo syllabus is structured as a series of 11 units. This book covers the first 9 of these units. (I propose to deal with the other units in a future book titled "Advanced Jo".) While these units are required from green belt onwards under the Muidokan syllabus, they can easily be adapted to any kyu system as shown in italics below:

Unit 1 – Green 1 (*9th kyu*)	Jo suburi (basics) 1-5 (thrusts) Kumijo 1 (2-person drill using suburi 1, 2 and 4)
Unit 2 – Green 2 (*8th kyu*)	Jo suburi (basics) 6-10 (strikes) Kumijo 2 (2-person drill using suburi 2, 5, 6 and 7)
Unit 3 – Green 3 (*7th kyu*)	Kumijo 3 (2-person drill using suburi 9 and 10)
Unit 4 – Green 4 (*6th kyu*)	Kumijo 4 (2-person drill using suburi 3, 5 and 8)
Unit 5 – Brown 1 (*5th kyu*)	Jo suburi (basics) 11-15 (wrist/shoulder movements) Kumijo 5 (2-person drill using suburi 11 and 15)
Unit 6 – Brown 2 (*4th kyu*)	Kumijo 6 (2-person drill using suburi 1 and 12)
Unit 7 – Brown 3 (*3rd kyu*)	Jo suburi (basics) 16-18 (movements from the shoulder) Kumijo 7 (2-person drill using suburi 1, 5, 13, 14 and 15)
Unit 8 – Brown 4 (*2nd kyu*)	Kumijo 8 (2-person drill using suburi 5, 14 and 16)
Unit 9 – Shodan 1 (*1st kyu*)	Jo suburi (basics) 19-20 (flowing movements) Kumijo 9 (2-person drill using suburi 19 and 20)
Unit 10 – Shodan 2 (*Shodan*)	Jusan jo kata (13 count kata that doubles as a 2-person drill)
Unit 11 – Nidan 1 (*Nidan*)	Sanjuichi jo kata (31 count kata)

GLOSSARY

aikido – a Japanese art of civilian defence founded by Morihei Ueshiba deriving mainly from the art of Daito ryu Aiki jujutsu

aikijo – the system of jodo used in aikido

choku zuki – a straight thrust

dachi – a stance

do/dao – the way (Japanese/Chinese)

gaeshi/kaeshi – a sweeping, circular movement

gedan – low height (eg. knees)

gedan gaeshi – a low sweeping strike to the knees, used in the third part of suburi 4 (see page 26) and 8 (see page 33) (see also **katate gedan gaeshi**)

gedan gaeshi evasion – the evasion comprising the second part of suburi 4 (see page 26)

gyaku – reverse

gyaku jodan sukui uke – a scooping head-height deflection that brushes the attack to the right (cf. jodan sukui uke which brushes the attack to the left) (see suburi 20 on page 52 and kumijo 9 on page 122 and 125)

gyaku yoko men uchi – strike to the side of the head

hachi – the number 8

harai – a circular movement

hasso – the shoulder

hasso gaeshi uke – the deflection used in the second part of suburi 13 (see page 38) and the first part of suburi 14 to 18 (see pages 40 to 46)

hasso no kamae – the guard posture used for shoulder-based techniques (see page 17)

hidari – the left

hikkake uke – a sideways brushing deflection with the jo held vertically, using the middle of the jo

jo – 4-foot staff

jodan – head height

jodan sukui uke – a circular "scooping" head height deflection (see page 29)

jodo – the "way of the jo" (ie. the art of fighting with the jo)

kaeshi uke – a curved deflection used in suburi 2 (see page 23)

kaeshi zuki – a thrust following a kaeshi uke, also the name of suburi 2 (see page 22)

kake uke – a hooking deflection

kamae – a preparatory or guard posture

kan – hall or school

katate – the wrist

katate gedan gaeshi – a low sweeping strike to the knee executed with the wrist used in suburi 11 (see page 36)

katate no kamae – a guard posture used for wrist techniques (see page 17)

kokutsu dachi – the back stance as described on page 15

kumijo – literally "a meeting of jos" but in this book it is a reference to the 2-person drills in Chapter 4

men – the head

migi – the right

Muidokan – the Japanese name for the Academy of Traditional Fighting Arts based in Perth, Australia

nagare – a flowing movement used in suburi 19 (see page 48) and 20 (see page 51)

neko ashi dachi – cat stance as described on page 13

"open" zenkutsu dachi – a zenkutsu dachi with the front foot turned out, as described on page 14

osae uke – a pressing deflection

renoji dachi – the main stance in jodo that forms a "tick" shape, as described on page 13

renzoku – consecutive

shiko dachi – the horse stance, as described on page 15

shomen – the front

shomen uchi – a downward strike to the front

suburi – basic techniques used in jodo (see Chapter 3)

sukui – a scooping movement

uchi – a strike

uchi no kamae – the guard posture used for strikes (see page 16)

uke – literally "to receive" but used to refer to deflections, parries or blocks

ushiro – to the rear

ushiro zuki – a thrust to the rear

wu-wei/mui – a Chinese/Japanese term from Daoist philosophy meaning "no unnatural action" and expressed in martial technique by movement along the lines of least resistance

yoko – the side

zenkutsu dachi – forward stance as described on page 14

zuki – a thrust

zuki no kamae – the guard posture used for thrusts (see page 16)

INDEX

ushiro zuki · 34, 35, 43, 44, 72, 78, 80, 82, 84, 86, 87, 114, 119, 120, 144

W

walking stick · 3
wu-wei · 4, 97, 108, 116, 125, 144

X

xingyi kun · 3
xingyiquan · 3, 135

Z

zenkutsu dachi · 13, 14, 21, 22, 30, 52, 75, 103, 115, 125, 143, 144
zuki no kamae · 15, 17, 21, 22, 24, 25, 27, 57, 71, 144

71732216R00089

Made in the USA
San Bernardino, CA
18 March 2018